Mountain Food Chains

Louise and Richard Spilsbury

Heinemann
LIBRARY

26869

 www.heinemann.co.uk/library
Visit our website to find out more information about Heinemann Library books.

To order:
 Phone 44 (0) 1865 888066
 Send a fax to 44 (0) 1865 314091
Visit the Heinemann Bookshop at www.heinemann.co.uk/library to browse our catalogue and order online.

First published in Great Britain by Heinemann Library, Halley Court, Jordan Hill, Oxford OX2 8EJ, part of Harcourt Education. Heinemann is a registered trademark of Harcourt Education Ltd.

Editorial: Sarah Eason and Kathy Peltan
Design: Jo Hinton-Malivoire and AMR
Picture Research: Ruth Blair and Ginny Stroud-Lewis
Illustration: Words and Publications
Production: Camilla Smith

Originated by Ambassador Litho Ltd
Printed in China by WKT Company Limited.

The paper used to print this book comes from sustainable resources.

ISBN 0 431 11904 X
09 08 07 06 05
10 9 8 7 6 5 4 3 2 1

British Library Cataloguing in Publication Data
Spilsbury, Louise and Richard
Food Chains: Mountains
557.5'316

A full catalogue record for this book is available from the British Library.

Acknowledgements
The Publishers would like to thank the following for permission to reproduce photographs:
Alamy p. **22**; a-z botanicals p. **17**; Corbis pp. **5** (David Muench), **7** (John M Roberts), **8**, **14**, **16** (Tom Brakefield), **10** (Galen Rowell), **15** (Gallo Images), **23** (Josef Polleross), **25** (John Van Hasselt), pp. **11**, **24**; Getty Images p. **27**; Heather Angel/Natural visions p. **12**; Nature PL pp. **13** (David Kjaer), **18** (Andrew Parkinson); Photodisk/Getty images p. **26**.

Cover photograph of a mountain hare eating red berries in the snow reproduced with permission of NHPA.

The Publishers would like to thank Michael Scott for his assistance in the preparation of this book.

Contents

Words in bold, **like this**, are explained in the Glossary.

What is a mountain food web?

Just as in all **habitats**, plants and animals that live and grow in a mountain habitat depend on each other for food. This is because all **organisms** eat or are eaten by other organisms. For example, in a mountain habitat rabbits eat grass and may themselves be eaten by eagles or foxes. When plants and animals die and rot they are eaten by other living things, such as insects, **fungi** and **bacteria**.

If you draw lines between each of the organisms that eat each other, you create a diagram called a food web. It is called a web because it looks rather like a tangled spider's web!

In food web diagrams, the arrows lead from the food to the animal that eats it.

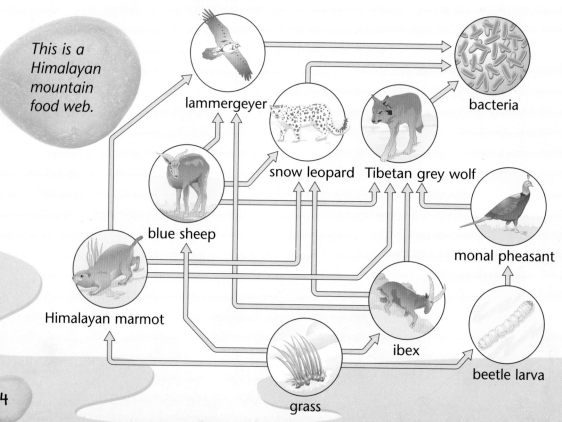

This is a Himalayan mountain food web.

lammergeyer

bacteria

snow leopard   Tibetan grey wolf

blue sheep

monal pheasant

Himalayan marmot

ibex

beetle larva

grass

These are rhododendrons, growing in the Black Mountains, eastern USA. These bushy plants with large flowers are found in different mountain areas of the world.

What are mountain habitats like?

Mountains are areas of land that are over 500 metres high – they are steeper and much higher than hills. Mountains are found all over the world. Even in warm countries, mountains can have snowy peaks because temperatures drop as you get higher in the air. Plants and animals that live in mountain habitats have to be especially suited or adapted to cope with the steep rocky slopes, harsh sunlight, fierce cold and strong winds found there.

All the organisms that live in mountain areas are part of a mountain food web. Some, such as mountain rabbits and hares, live there all year round. Others, such as hummingbirds or American redstarts, visit mountains at certain times of year when there is plenty of food that they like to eat.

What is a mountain food chain?

Food webs may look complicated at first sight, but they are made up of simpler food chains. Food chain diagrams show **organisms** that eat each other as links in a single chain. They follow the movement of food and **energy** as it passes from one link to another. The arrows in a food chain diagram show which direction the energy moves in.

Most plants and animals are part of more than one food chain because they eat or are eaten by more than one kind of organism. Animals that eat different kinds of food usually have a greater chance of survival than those that rely on just one kind of food. If an animal relied on one food source and that food supply ran out, the animal would starve.

This diagram of a mountain food chain shows how energy passes from one link in the chain to another.

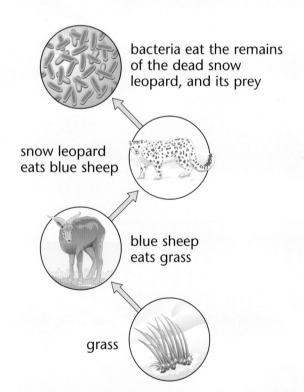

bacteria eat the remains of the dead snow leopard, and its prey

snow leopard eats blue sheep

blue sheep eats grass

grass

*The plants in this mountain **habitat** are a vital source of energy for all other organisms that live there. Only plants can trap energy from sunlight.*

Starting the chain

The Sun is the source of energy for almost all the living things on Earth. Plants are able to capture some of the energy in sunlight in their leaves. They use it to make their own food from carbon dioxide (a gas in the air) and water, in a process called **photosynthesis**.

As well as food, plants need small amounts of **nutrients** from the soil. They absorb these nutrients, along with water, through their roots.

Animals cannot get energy from the Sun – they get their energy from food. Some animals get energy by eating parts of plants. By eating plants they gain some of the energy stored within them. For example, mountain hares eat grass leaves, birds eat tree berries. **Decomposers** such as **fungi** and **bacteria**, then feed on dead plants and animals.

Making the chain

Food chains start with a **producer**. Plants are known as producers because they produce (make) food. Animals are **consumers**. They cannot make their own food. They have to consume (eat) plants or other organisms to get energy.

Herbivores are animals that feed mainly on plant parts, such as leaves, seeds or berries. In food chains herbivores are called **primary consumers**, because they are the first ones to gain energy from the plants. **Carnivores** are animals that eat other animals. Carnivores are known as **secondary consumers**, because they consume some of the plant's energy only after another animal has eaten it. Secondary consumers catch and eat primary consumers and other secondary consumers. **Omnivores** are animals that eat both plants and other animals. They are primary and secondary consumers.

The mountain lion is a carnivore, or secondary consumer. It often eats herbivores like this snowshoe hare.

More links in the chain

Food chains do not end when organisms eventually die. **Scavengers** are animals that eat the dead remains of other animals. In mountain habitats, scavengers can be large, like vultures, or small, like worms or insects. Decomposers such as bacteria and fungi eat any dead remains not taken by scavengers. Decomposers break the remains into tiny pieces. Some pieces become food for the decomposers, while some get washed into the soil and become nutrients for plants. When new plants absorb these nutrients through their roots and use them to grow, the food chain begins again!

This diagram shows the movement of energy in a mountain food chain, from plant producer, to primary consumer, and on to the secondary consumer and decomposer.

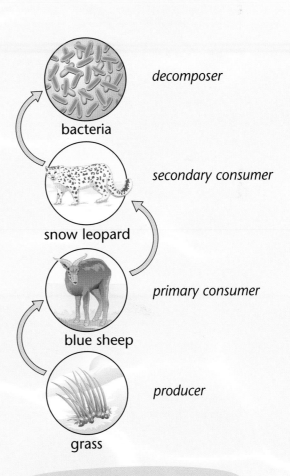

decomposer

bacteria

secondary consumer

snow leopard

primary consumer

blue sheep

producer

grass

Scavengers and decomposers have between them reduced this blue sheep to little more than bones.

Breaking the chain

All of the organisms in a food web are connected to each other and their habitat. If some of the organisms die out, it may prove disastrous for others in their food web.

Sometimes natural events can damage a habitat and the food webs that exist within it. Avalanches are when large amounts of snow, ice and rock slip down a mountain. An avalanche can knock down large areas of forest on the mountainside, destroying the habitat for many animals and plants, but creating open areas that other **species** can use until the trees eventually grow back. Human activity, such as taking over mountain land for buildings, can also cause breaks in mountain food chains and webs. When people disturb wild habitats and create **pollution**, some of the organisms within the habitat may die.

Which producers live in mountains?

On mountains, as in all other **habitats** on Earth, plants are the **producers**. Different kinds of producers live at different heights up mountains. Lower slopes, where it is usually warmer and less windy, may be coated with dense rainforests or stands of broad-leaved trees. On higher slopes there are **coniferous** trees, which can survive in colder temperatures.

At a certain point up a high mountain, it becomes too cold and windy for trees to grow. Above this **tree line**, tough, low-growing plants such as heather and grasses thrive. The highest parts of some mountains look like rocky wasteland. Most of the small plants that grow here huddle in sheltered gaps between rocks. **Lichens** live on bare rock faces. These are especially tough **fungi** that have tiny plant-like **organisms** called **algae** living inside them. In return for shelter, the algae produce food for the fungi!

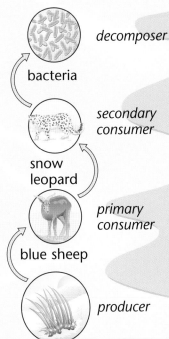

decomposer

bacteria

secondary consumer

snow leopard

primary consumer

blue sheep

producer

grass

Can you see the tree line on this mountain?

This colourful flowering plant grows high in the Himalayan mountains. Many mountain flowering plants grow in sheltered spots, protected from the cold and wind by the surrounding rock.

Mountain flowers

One of the ways in which many flowering plants cope with mountain life is by growing close to the ground, out of the path of icy winds. Some have fine hair-like strands on their leaves and stems to trap a layer of warm air around them. They often have very colourful, highly scented flowers to attract the few **pollinators**, such as bumblebees, that fly in mountainous areas. In **temperate** areas, many flowering plants survive cold winters underground in seeds or bulbs and emerge in spring and summer. In higher, colder mountain regions, summers are very short. Plants grow, flower and make their seeds in just two or three months.

Breaking the chain: producers

Trees are a vital part of many mountain food chains. In the Andes Mountains of South America, the seeds of Polylepis trees are the main food of Cochabamba mountain finches. People chop down Polylepis trees for firewood. With less Polylepis seed to eat, the finches are getting rarer – there are just 2500 adults left. **Predators** that eat the finches, such as falcons, then have less **prey** to eat.

Which primary consumers live in mountains?

Mountain **primary consumers** eat many different kinds of plants. Some are more fussy than others. Bighorn sheep in the USA eat anything from grass and bark to moss, whereas giant pandas in China eat only particular kinds of bamboo plants. Small mountain **herbivores** may eat different parts of plants. Mountain pine beetle **larvae** live under pine tree bark feeding on sweet sap in the wood. Hummingbirds, bees and moths fly from flower to flower in search of rich sources of **nectar** or **pollen** to eat.

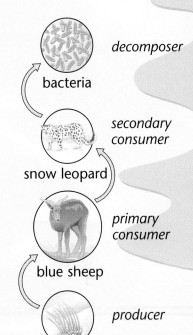

decomposer
bacteria

secondary consumer
snow leopard

primary consumer
blue sheep

producer
grass

Large mountain herbivores

Some mountain primary consumers are large **mammals**. Mountain zebras in southwestern Africa eat grass. They may spend half of each day grazing, to get enough **energy** from their plant food. Mountain gorillas eat around 40 different kinds of plants, including vines, thistles and wild celery.

Capercaillies are ground-living mountain birds that feed mostly on bilberry plants and pine needles.

Mountain goats and hares

Mountain mammals usually have thick fur to protect them from the cold and wind as they search for food. Mountain goats have woolly hair for warmth. Their tough hooves protect their feet as they climb amongst hard rock crags looking for plant twigs and moss to eat. Mountain hares grow white fur in winter so **predators** cannot see them so easily against the snow as they search for grass or heather leaves to eat.

Mountain rodents

Many mountain primary consumers, such as pikas and marmots, are **rodents** that live in underground burrows and come out to feed. Pikas eat leaves. In autumn they collect leaves and spread them out to dry before piling them in their burrows. Dry leaves last the winter better than wet leaves, so their food stores last longer.

*Marmots spend most of the year eating the leaves and flowers of many different plants and grasses. They **hibernate** in winter when food is scarce.*

Which secondary consumers live in mountains?

Secondary consumers are animals that get their **energy** by eating other animals. Some are **predators** that use a lot of energy to chase and catch **prey** in mountain **habitats**. Others are **scavengers** that feed on dead animals.

Mountain birds of prey

Birds of prey are birds that hunt other animals to eat. They can soar over all levels of a mountain searching for food. Peregrine falcons and eagles hunt for birds in the sky and small **mammals** on the ground. Some birds such as vultures and condors are scavengers. Their wide wings allow them to soar on the breezes blowing up mountains as they look out for dead animals.

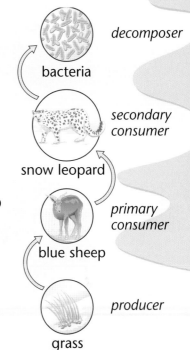

decomposer
bacteria

secondary consumer
snow leopard

primary consumer
blue sheep

producer
grass

The lammergeyer is a mountain scavenger that often feeds on mammal skeletons. It carries bones into the air and drops them on to rocks to get at the juicy **marrow** inside.

Mountain cats and dogs

The snow leopard is a rare mountain cat that hunts wild sheep and goats, marmots, hares and birds. The mountain lion, also known as a cougar or puma, is also a kind of cat. It measures about two metres long and it eats large mammals such as deer and wild pigs. Some members of the dog family, such as foxes and coyotes, also live and feed on mountains. Both hunt mainly rabbits, hares and **rodents**, but may also scavenge on dead animals.

Coyotes usually hunt alone for small prey like this mouse, but they sometimes hunt larger prey in packs.

Breaking the chain: secondary consumers

In parts of western North America where people have killed wolves, elk have increased in number because they have no **predators**. The elk then eat so many plants from the edge of mountain rivers that they reduce the shade that some kinds of fish use to feed and shelter in. So killing the wolves reduced the number of fish.

Which decomposers live in mountains?

Decomposers are living things that feed on the remains of other **organisms**. Dead plants and animals and their waste rot because decomposers break them down. When these remains rot, **nutrients** are released. Decomposers take in some of the nutrients, but others are released into the soil. Trees and other plants can take in these nutrients through their roots and use them to grow, so starting new food chains and webs. Mountain decomposers include **fungi** and **bacteria**. Many live in the soil or shelter under rocks or plants.

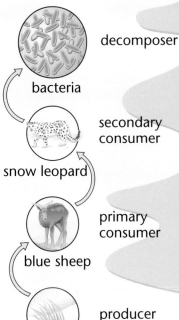

decomposer

bacteria

secondary consumer

snow leopard

primary consumer

blue sheep

producer

grass

Fungi

Fungi grow thin threads called hyphae through dead wood and other plant parts. The hyphae make chemicals that rot the waste around them. Then the fungi can absorb some of these plant nutrients. In some mountain **habitats**, web-cap fungi live amongst the fallen leaves that build up under trees such as dwarf willows and pine trees.

Pine trees rely on fungi such as web-caps to recycle nutrients from their dead leaves.

Bacteria

Even in thin mountain soils there are millions of miniscule bacteria in the ground. Most of these bacteria live in thin films of water trapped around the particles (tiny bits) of soil. Some feed on chemicals such as proteins that are found in the bodies of living things. Others feed on the waste products of other bacteria.

Animals that help decomposers

When some animals eat dead organisms or animal waste, they help break them down into smaller bits that decomposers can use. These mini-**scavengers** include worms and insects such as maggots and beetles. Springtails are tiny insects that can survive under snow on mountaintops, where there is virtually nothing alive or growing. They scrape a living by eating dead insects, fungi and other waste that blows there on the wind.

*Dung beetles lay their eggs on animal dung. The beetle **larvae** feed on the dung when they hatch. This helps break down waste, so decomposers can get to work.*

How are mountain food chains different in different places?

Food chains can be very different from one mountain to another. Mountain food chains are affected by **climate**, the height of the mountain and the amount of human activity in the area.

Mount Kenya

Mount Kenya is Africa's second highest mountain at 5200 metres (17,060 feet) high. On the lower slopes the **producers** are rainforest trees, while higher up there are areas of bamboo. Higher still is open ground with fewer plants.

The **primary consumers** in the forests include elephants, bushbuck and bongo antelopes, all of which eat grass, leaves and twigs. Black and white colobus monkeys eat tree leaves. Hyraxes are small **herbivores** that clamber up rock outcrops using sticky pads on their feet. Olive baboons are **omnivores** that eat fruit, grass and roots, but also animal food such as insects and bird eggs. **Secondary consumers** include cats such as servals, that eat birds and hyraxes, and leopards, which hunt larger **prey** such as bushbucks, colobus monkeys and olive baboons.

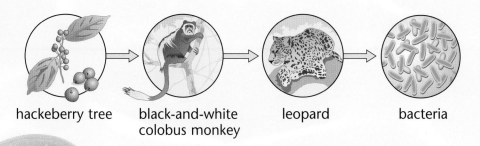

hackeberry tree   black-and-white   leopard   bacteria
                   colobus monkey

This is just one of many Mount Kenya food chains.

The Alps

The Alps is a huge mountain range in Europe. Its highest mountain is Mont Blanc at 4807 metres (15,770 feet). High Alpine areas are made up of steep cliffs and fallen rock with little plant life. Even so, there are many food chains here.

The chamois is a kind of goat that jumps from rock to rock on its hoofed feet, feeding on patches of flowers, moss and **lichen**. The lynx, a kind of wild cat, is one of its **predators**. Groups of marmots live in burrows and feed on grass. When a group of marmots is feeding, one of them watches out for predators such as **birds of prey**.

Griffon vultures and maggots (fly **larvae**) are Alpine **scavengers**. They eat the flesh of dead animals, such as chamois, that they find on the slopes. **Bacteria** slowly decay any remains they leave behind.

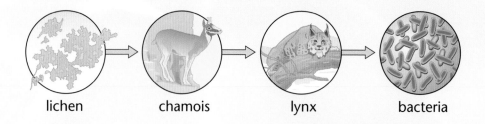

| lichen | chamois | lynx | bacteria |

*This shows a food chain in an Alpine mountain **habitat**.*

The Rocky Mountains

The awesome Rocky Mountains run for almost 5000 kilometres through North America, from Alaska to Mexico. Many different primary consumers, such as mountain goats and marmots, eat grasses and other small producers for much of the year. Birds such as grouse and **mammals** from small snowshoe hares to enormous moose, feast on the small, **energy**-rich berries of shrubs such as mountain cranberry in autumn.

Bobcats (relatives of the lynx) and golden eagles are secondary consumers of snowshoe hares, marmots and grouse. Some of the largest predators in the Rockies are omnivores. Black bears eat small prey such as marmots, fish and insects, but also roots and berries.

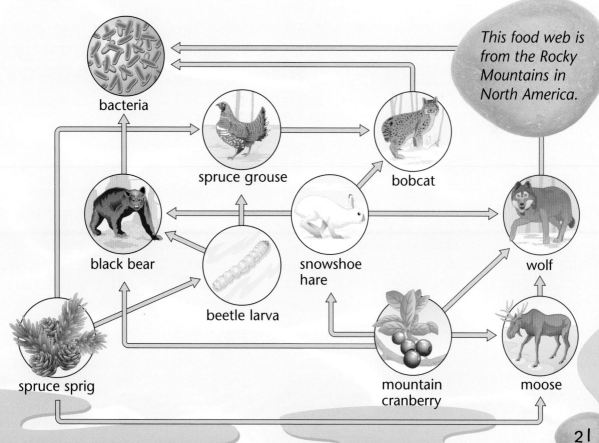

This food web is from the Rocky Mountains in North America.

bacteria

spruce grouse

bobcat

black bear

beetle larva

snowshoe hare

wolf

spruce sprig

mountain cranberry

moose

What happens to a food web when a food chain breaks down?

Many mountain food chains and webs around the world are under threat because of human activities. When people affect a single link in a food chain in a **habitat**, it can affect many other links of that food chain and the whole food web. The effects are much greater when whole areas of habitat are damaged.

Habitat destruction

Mountain forests are being cut down for timber, and to clear land for farming and mining. Loss of mountain forests in northern Europe means there is little food and shelter for rare European bears. Miners in the Appalachians in the USA are destroying mountain peaks to get at the coal below. In the process they have destroyed large areas of forest that are home to birds such as water thrushes. They have also filled in or **polluted** mountain streams killing fish, **amphibians** and insects.

Large areas of mountain forest in Oregon, USA, have been cut down for timber.

This huge litter dump was made by tourists visiting Mount Sinai in Israel.

Cutting down mountain forests can lead to further disaster. Trees stop soil and snow from slipping down steep mountain slopes. When there are fewer trees, there are more destructive landslides and avalanches.

Tourism

For some people living in mountain areas, visitors can be a good thing. They provide work in tourist industries, such as hotels. However, tourists may drop litter, pollute water and use up firewood. Mountain walkers and climbers wear away paths and some accidentally start fires that can destroy large areas of plants and small animals.

Acid rain

When people burn fuels, especially in factories or vehicle engines, they release polluting gases. These mix with rainwater to make acid rain. Acid rain damages mountain lakes, killing fish within them, and destroys leaves on mountain forest trees, removing the **producer** link from many food chains.

The ice cliffs around Glacier Bay in Alaska, USA are melting as a result of global warming.

Climate change

Scientists believe that the world's **climate** is changing. A layer of polluting gases in the atmosphere, produced by power stations, factories and cars, is trapping the Sun's heat. The resulting global rise in temperature affects mountains in different ways. For example, in the Rocky Mountains of Canada, pine-beetles that eat pine leaves used to die out in cold winters. Warmer winters have meant pine-beetles have increased in numbers and they have killed vast areas of mountain forest.

Breaking the chain: unwanted additions

Food chains can be broken if a new **organism** is introduced to a habitat. Giant wetas, the world's heaviest insects, are found in some New Zealand mountains. These flightless **herbivores** are now rare, mostly because many have been killed by animals that people brought to New Zealand, such as dogs and ferrets.

How can we protect mountain food chains?

Around the world, people are working to protect mountain **habitats** and the living things that make up mountain food chains and webs.

Scientists study mountain habitats to see how changes there affect plants and animals. For example, scientists studying Mount Kilimanjaro in Tanzania discovered that there is much less ice and snow at the top of the mountain than there used to be. With less snow to melt into water and flow into streams and rivers, mountain and river wildlife has been affected.

In the 1980s scientists found that the number of snow leopards in the Himalayan Mountains was decreasing. People were illegally hunting both the snow leopards and animals such as antelope that the snow leopards usually feed on. The scientists encouraged the Chinese government to establish the Chang Tang Wildlife Preserve in nearby Tibet in 1993 to protect these animals.

*At the Italian Research Centre in Nepal, scientists study how **climate** change is affecting the amount of snow on Mount Everest.*

Conservation groups

Conservation groups are organizations that work to protect the natural world and the plants and animals that live in it. Many conservation groups are charities that raise money from ordinary people to fund their work. International conservation groups include WWF and Friends of the Earth. They carry out research and campaign to raise public awareness about issues, such as the destruction of mountain habitats and the problems facing **endangered species**, such as European wolves and the Iberian lynx.

Conservation groups also run projects to educate people living on or near mountains about how they can help to protect the habitat. For example, in the Himalayas, conservation groups are encouraging people not to cut down trees and shrubs to burn as fuel, but to use an oil called kerosene to cook with instead.

This conservationist is planting trees to help restore a mountain habitat.

Research a mountain food web

You can research your own mountain food chains and webs. You could use information from this and other books and sources on the Internet. When you are working on your food chains, think about the factors that affect what lives there. For example, is the habitat hot or cold, wet or dry? Here are some other things to think about when making food chains.

1. What are the plant **producers** in the habitat?
2. What animals live there? Try to group them – which are the insects, birds and **mammals**, for example.
3. What does each animal eat?
4. Which are the **predators** and which are the **prey**?
5. Link some of the different **organisms** together in food chains and then combine them in a food web.

If you visit a mountain habitat, think about the food chains there. Try to stick to paths, to avoid eroding mountainsides or disturbing wildlife. This hiker is trekking toward Mt. Ama Dablam in the Himalayan mountains.

Where are the world's main mountains?

The map on these pages shows you where some of the major mountain ranges in the world are located.

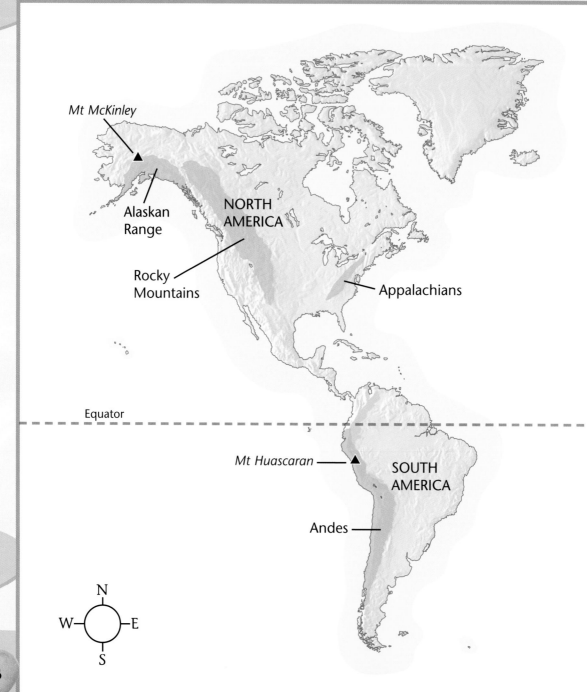

Mt McKinley

Alaskan Range

NORTH AMERICA

Rocky Mountains

Appalachians

Equator

Mt Huascaran

SOUTH AMERICA

Andes

N
W — E
S

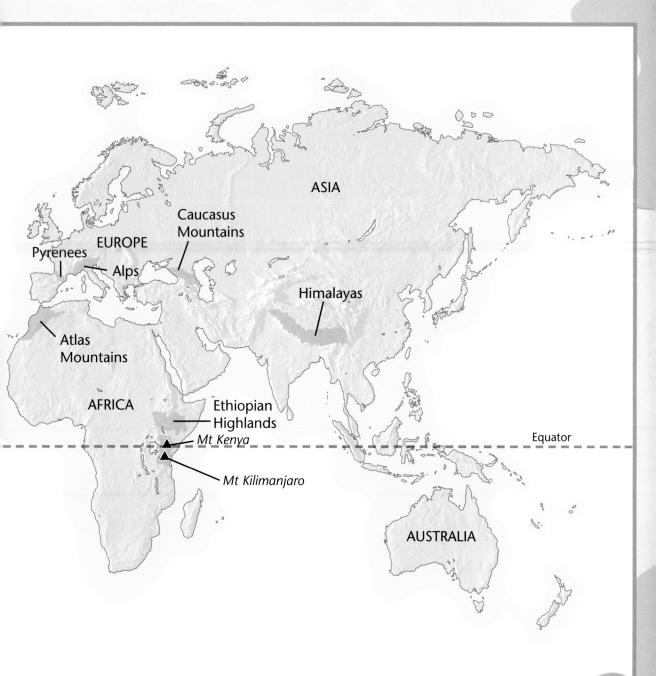

ASIA

Caucasus
Mountains

EUROPE

Pyrenees

Alps

Himalayas

Atlas
Mountains

AFRICA

Ethiopian
Highlands

Mt Kenya

Equator

Mt Kilimanjaro

AUSTRALIA

Glossary

algae (singular alga) small plant-like organisms

amphibians group of animals which breed in water but live part of their life on land

bacteria (singular bacterium) tiny living decomposers found everywhere

bird of prey bird that hunts animals for food

carnivore animal that eats the flesh of another animal

climate the general conditions of weather in an area

coniferous trees such as pine and fir that usually have needle-like leaves and produce their seeds in cones

consumers organisms that eat other organisms

decomposers organisms that break down and get nutrients from dead plants and animals and their waste

endangered when a species of animal or plant is in danger of dying out completely

energy power to grow, move and do things

fungi group of decomposer organisms including mushrooms, toadstools and their relatives

habitat place where an organism lives

herbivore animal that eats plants

hibernate go into a special long sleep to avoid bad weather and scarce food

larvae (singular larva) the young of some insects and other animals

lichens group of low-growing organisms made up of fungi and algae living together

mammals group of animals that feed their babies on milk from their own bodies

marrow rich 'jelly' inside bones

nectar sugary substance made by plants to attract insects, which eat it

nutrients chemicals that plants and animals need to live

omnivore animal that eat both plants and other animals

organism living thing

photosynthesis process by which plants make their own food using carbon dioxide (a gas in the air), water and energy from sunlight

pollen small grains that are the male parts of a flower. Pollen combines with eggs (female flower parts) to form seeds.

pollinator insect that carries pollen from the male part of a flower to the female part

polluted poisoned or made dirty by substances produced by human activities

predators animals that hunt and eat other animals

prey animals that are caught and eaten by predators

primary consumers animals that eat plants

producer organism (plant) that can make its own food

rodents mammals with large gnawing front teeth, such as mice and rats

scavengers organisms that feed on dead plants and animals, and waste

secondary consumers animals that eat primary consumers and other secondary consumers

species group of organisms that are very similar and can breed together to produce young

temperate belonging to a region of the world that has warm summers and cold, wet winters

tree line the height on a mountain above which it is too cold and windy for trees to grow

tropical belonging to a region of the world that is warm all year round but has one or more rainy seasons

Find out more

Books and CD-Roms

Cycles in Nature: Food Chains, Theresa Greenaway (Hodder Wayland/Raintree Steck-Vaughn, 2001)

Science Answers: Food Chains and Webs, Louise and Richard Spilsbury (Heinemann Library, 2004)

Taking Action: WWF, Louise Spilsbury (Heinemann Library, 2000)

Food Chains and Webs CD-ROM (Heinemann Library, 2004) has supporting interactive activities and video clips.

Websites

Find out about the work of conservation groups in helping mountain habitats and the organisms that live there at:

www.wwf.org.uk   WWF-UK
www.wwf.org.au   WWF Australia
www.foe.co.uk   Friends of the Earth UK
www.foe.org.au   Friends of the Earth Australia.

Learn about mountain forests in Canada and have a go at constructing a food chain at:
www.borealforest.org/school/food_chain.htm

Index

Titles in the *Food Chains and Webs* series include:

Hardback   0 431 11903 1

Hardback   0 431 11905 8

Hardback   0 431 11904 X

Hardback   0 431 11902 3

Hardback   0 431 11901 5

Hardback   0 431 11900 7

Find out about the other titles in this series on our website www.heinemann.co.uk/library